sofisticatedwhitetrash

Sofisticated White Trash

selected poems by

J.J. CAMPBELL

INTERIOR NOISE PRESS
Austin, Texas USA

Sofisticated White Trash
Copyright © 2013 by J.J. Campbell

All rights reserved. Printed in the United States of America. No part of this book may be used or reproduced in any manner whatsoever without written permission except in the case of brief quotations embodied in critical articles and reviews.

For order information and current mailing address please visit www.interiornoisepress.com

Interior Noise Press
Austin, TX

Book Design by David p Bates

Library of Congress Control Number: 2013933960

ISBN 978-0-9816606-8-4
First Edition

*to the woman of my dreams,
hopefully we will meet one day.*

contents

5 pm in ohio and it suddenly all makes sense
a bedtime story
a crossroads of sorts
a day in the life
a long road to redemtion
a matter of convenience
a pain like no other
a symphony
a younger woman
a quarter century of failure
all eyes on me
all my creative juices
american flag
an endless trail of pain
and suddenly it felt like i was in thailand
another roadside cross
awkward
back when i was nineteen and immortal
beauty queens
birthdays
boyish good looks
burning bridges
child like innocence

chocolate cake for breakfast
classical music
columbus day
convict pussy
dangling from the rooftops again
discarded
down in a hole
driving
ellen barkin
envy
even hell and back
fleeting at best
from my empty bed
games
hatred
homeless
hoping this tension will bring the truth
i have the scars to prove it
i woke up this morning
i hate my father
i like my mom better anyway
idle thoughts on a sunday night
in the local section
in the valley of this connected generation

irony
junkies of death
just another sweaty fat fuck
kung fu theater of the mind
like a fading kiss
like it nearly had a meaning
living in my stereo(type)
making a list, checking it twice
mission accomplished
molly ringwald
my ball of energy
my father's sentiments on my 18th birthday
my life in a black high school
my luck with the ladies
my personal pam grier
nothing but the dog in me
now i believe
on my porch
on the curve of your hips
one for isabella
only your imagination
our hero tattooed in black lace
paralyze
patiently waiting at the station

performance anxiety

pleasure often brings pain

priorities

ramblings of a long winded ass clown

sadness, through male eyes

safety first

sara

saving the world from a future ungrateful bastard

she did say i was cute though

she refused to drink it

social anxiety disorder

sometimes i wish i was pink

sour milk on fruit loops

stink

strike up the band

stuck here in the cold silence

suicide watch

the american dream

the bitch with the black eye

the cruel circle of lonliness

the enigma

the outskirts of downtown

the rapture

the shallow end of the gene pool

the unexpected death of an old friend
the urinal for little boys
the wheels on the bus go round and round
the spark of my youth
think before speaking
this lovely mess
this silly episode called life
time has been much kinder to her
trash
tuesday afternoon sex
unemployment
untitled grief on a september afternoon
up by the big barn
welcome to the small press kid
what is rain
while masturbating today
wish you were here
wishful thinking
with no peaceful resolution in sight
withdrawn
within five minutes of entering the supermarket
yet another pitiful day
you can only watch the same movie so many times
your wall of regret

The most dangerous creation of any society is the man who has nothing to lose.

James A. Baldwin

5 pm in ohio and it suddenly all makes sense

another night hunting
for inspiration in
empty bottles

fading tail lights
down an old dirt
road

there's no lust left
in your kiss

no desire emerging
from your eyes
anymore

passion must have
got on that bus as
well

my rekindled faith
reminded me that
hope was lost long
ago

it shall rain for days
on end now that the
harvest has come to
pass

everything seems
slightly out of step
and no one is
beyond reproach

a bedtime story

every night i close my
eyes i see a lemon
flavored hatred hidden
behind every door

your candy lips
trace a bloody
outline of my soul

our perfection is now a
blackened lung

and in the silence of a
full moon we both can
hear every heart break

we'll meet again

some lonesome day

some old abandoned
town

west of the guilt river

down by where the
future is buried

goodnight my princess

you shall be missed

a crossroads of sorts

another new
year

another list
of resolutions
for the recycle
pile

another lonely
beer

another ball
drop with no
one to kiss

i will soon be
37 and at a
crossroads of
sorts

on one hand do
i take that hand
and ball it up into
a fist and beat
myself to death

or on the other
hand do i keep
on pretending
i'm this cool
motherfucker
who never panics
and is fine no
matter what

another question
that i'll simply

wait to find out
the answer to

either way
someone is
going to be

bitterly
disappointed

a day in the life

it was one of those rare occasions
that i actually left my cage

you know
for a few odds and ends
some rays of sunshine
a breath of fresh air
or whatever fucking reason
people go out these days

and it was as soon as i
entered the store that i realized
why i don't leave my cage
very often anymore

the purses were held a bit
closer to the chest
children stared and then ran
back to inattentive parents
the quick double glances
followed by hushed voices
"did you see that fucking guy?!"

it felt like my adolescence
all over again
the weirdo, the outcast
the misunderstood non-conformist
the echoes of counselors and parents
"we just don't see why you don't
want to fit in"

as this mini-movie was
playing in my head
i put some milk in my cart
a woman strolled past me
that smelled rather nice

instead of playing it cool
and saying "excuse me, what's that
lovely perfume you're wearing?"
i sniffed rather loudly
trying to get all of the scent
out of the air

she stopped, looked back at me
gave me that what the fuck
are you doing look

i smiled and she looked away
she walked quickly to
the other end of the store

i began laughing to myself
thought the world was getting
back to normal

i proceeded to the checkout lane
stared off into the distance
watched the people come and go
wondered if one of them
could possibly be carrying
a loaded gun

i suppose at the time
the wonder was actually a wish

to my disappointment
i made it out of there alive
minus the money for my items
and the time it took to
weave my path through
the creatures

the wanna be trendy teenagers

the anorexic mothers
the soon to be gay stock boys
and of course, the old women

the old women who make me,
out of the fear that i truly am
a violent motherfucker deep within,
yearn for the comfort of my cage
the very second
i step out of it

a long road to redemption

i'm slowly drowning here in my
inability to chase away my past

my cousin's teenage nipples
in my mouth at age four

my father's hands wrapped
around my neck as i prayed
to pass out and die

the first time i got a rope, a
ladder and thought about
climbing a tree

the night i drank a bottle of
nyquil and decided to light
a bonfire

the smell of burning flesh
is still fresh in my mind

the joy of being the white kid
in my part black part nigger
part white childhood in a
forgotten suburb

to finding the right one only to
find out that she likes girls

to finding the other right one
only to realize that you work
better together as friends

that is until the fiancée is
uncomfortable with the
knowledge that the best
friend once had his dick
in the soon to be wife's ass

drinking and driving

searching for a cheap thrill

an easy whore that can cough

a gun that won't get jammed

but this solitary road is filled
with forks and you can rest
assured i've taken nothing but
wrong paths

the therapy never worked

the alcohol turned into torture
for pleasure

and i'm too poor to afford the drugs

closing in on thirty

my hope is fading like paint on
a car deserted in the sun

it's a long road to redemption when
you have no fucking desire to walk
the path at all

let alone trying to do it with only
the help of past demons, yes people
and fellow tortured souls that
wouldn't mind a death sealed with
hollywood approval

thank god i was blessed with good
looks, an athletic body and a silver
spoon in my mouth

fuck

that's the imaginary friend of my
youth i'm thinking of

i bet that fucker still gets more
pussy than me

the bastard

didn't even have the courtesy to take
me along when he made his escape

a matter of convenience

they're building a funeral home
right across the street from
the local nursing home

all in the spirit of
one-stop shopping
i imagine

a pain like no other

there was a sad
consolation in her
voice that sent a
chill down my spine

she went on to tell me
about how she tried to
kill herself earlier in
the day

and i, trying to be some
voice of some bizarre
kind of reason asked if
she views this as a failure
or as a sign of something
that wasn't meant to be

and with a numbing
bitterness she muttered
failure

and it was right then that
i knew my good friend
would kill herself

maybe not today, maybe
not in a few weeks but at
the end of the day i can
see that she sees no other
way out

so, just in case i never
get the chance let me
take this time to say
i love you

take care my friend

godspeed

a quarter century of failure

this year roughly marks twenty
five years since i first had the
notion to kill myself

how does one celebrate
such an anniversary

shotgun

alcohol

razor blades
and a bathtub

a running car
in a closed
garage

a vacation to
the golden gate
bridge

it's a shame that all of
them ring so hollow
and are so clichéd

sadly i think it's the
current path for me
letting the beard grow
and simply fading away

leaving it to the rest of
you to come up with a
better cliché

though, i will warn you now
if i happen to come into some
money i'm hiring a firing squad

i've always been a big fan of
history and god knows i could
use another last cigarette

a symphony

a friend of mine told me
that having sex with this woman
was like listening to a symphony
and being a fan of classical music
i decided to pursue it

so after a few days
of prodding and begging
dinner and a few bullshit lines
i finally got her into bed

and she reminded me of beethoven
when she took off her clothes
it was like the beginning of his 5th
loud, boisterous, and it knocked
me right on my ass
but like most of beethoven
my mind began to wander
in the middle

so i flipped her over
and began conducting myself
my tongue danced
the moonlight sonata in her mouth
while i pounded his 9th
into her soul

she climaxed to the ode to joy
so like any good conductor
i took a bow
made a drink and began
smoking a cigarette
thinking about my next piece
of music

a younger woman

>don't cum
>in my mouth
>i have rules
>she said
>
>and here i
>thought fucking
>around with a
>younger woman
>was going to
>be fun

all eyes on me

i've thought about putting racing stripes
and flames on my black 96 saturn
four doors, family sedan,
tape deck and factory speakers

and if i did that, i might as well
get the new sound system so i can
blast joe walsh as i drive around
this small town

i used to hate their stares and
dirty glances, but not anymore

all eyes on me motherfucker

i love it, crave it and it's good
for my budding insane ego

i have to watch it though
the cops here already hate me
and i'm sure there's some old law
on the books saying they can ban me
from their utopia if they please

it certainly wouldn't surprise me
if there was such a law
given that no black people
live in this town

maybe i'll pick up some old n.w.a.
when i get the amp for the speakers

all my creative juices

i've grown
tired of
waiting for
miracles

and i'm
not above
paying for
it

yet here i
am

five fucking
years since
my dick saw
something
other than
my left hand

my complete
inability to
give a shit has
a tremendous
grip on this
dying soul

and all my
creative juices
are wasted on
these lovely
beauties that
grace my tv
screen

i imagined
death would
always be

more painful
than this

american flag
September 19, 2001

      i have never put an
      american flag on my
      house or in my yard

      unlike most americans
      i could never turn the
      blind eye to the
      atrocities that have been
      committed under that flag

      and now
      unlike the majority of
      these suddenly patriotic
      hypocritical masses

      i will not place
      an american flag
      on my car, or in my yard
      or paint it on the
      side of my house

      my refusal to do so
      is due to
      what i imagine to be
      all the atrocities yet to come

an endless trail of pain

the neon lights of my youth are crushed
stuffed in some dumpster on the underside
of the world

the happiness i've always yearned for
turned out to be an endless trail of pain

broken dreams trapped in a brown bottle

and i can close my eyes and see the kid
wearing the purple shoes

walking the downtown streets without a care

smoking with the homeless, pissing away
daddy's money on alcohol and pot

completely sure that one day brilliance
would shine through

yet here i am

depressed and lost

left asking a god that doesn't care why

the gun closet gets closer every night i
cry myself to sleep

but i find myself waiting

want to make sure those last words
don't disappoint

and the sarcastic fucker inside me knows
no one has anything to fear

i haven't written anything good in years

besides, my lock picking skills aren't
what they used to be

a doctor told me the other day if i go
on a drinking binge i may very well die

thank god hardly anyone
remembers dylan thomas

and suddenly it felt like i was in thailand

i was jerking off to
some hot little asian
girl the other night
on the tv

she began to talk about
how she always felt like
a girl and when she had
her operation to become
one

the dilemma smacked
me right across the face

was i morally outraged
enough to stop?

was i weirded out too
much to continue?

was i in need of the
remote post haste?

well, thank god for a
creative imagination
and a complete lack
of morals

besides, i was a good
30 strokes past any
kind of shame i could
have imagined

another roadside cross

two teens died in
a car wreck about
a mile away from
my farm

i want to tell the
parents they should
be thankful their kids
died long before they
could grow up to be
disappointments like
most other children
in this town

but that would be
mean spirited
and true

and no one wants
the truth while
grieving

awkward

my
favorite
online
stripper
goes by
the same
nickname
as my
sister

somewhere
freud is
smiling

back when i was nineteen and immortal

another day full of clouds, rain and fog
like some depressing movie my mind
has conjured up, probably with fucking
subtitles since all my other personalities
are drunken bastards from foreign lands

and it's days like these that make me
long for the days of a cigarette dangling
from my lips as i try to listen to some
college radio in between the static of
talk radio and some shitty country
music channel that played the
commercial for the gun and knife show
every ten minutes

back when i was nineteen and immortal

knew every goddamn thing there was
to know and was still looked at as
somewhat desirable by the opposite sex

40 to 50 pounds and damn
near a decade ago now

back when loneliness didn't drip from
my pores, when the desperation to die
was nothing more than a night of
heavy drinking

but the constant longing has left
me short on today, on the now,
on what i've been running from
to find nothing new here in
my waste

and every time i try to walk out
on this movie it's like trying to
wake from the sleep of death

trapped in this 3D box of life

knowing sooner or later my life is
going to end up in my own hands
and it won't be pretty

my friends think i'm crazy to think
one day i'll end up on a street bench
covered in newspaper, rotting away

they would think that though

these poor over medicated souls
caught between mental health
and whatever trendy drug the
industry is pushing this month

i pray for them much more
than i pray for myself or the
rest of the world

time to shave my head
and find a new addiction

something the chicks will dig
before i end up as the creepy
fuck on the news arrested in
the schoolyard for trying to
find a way back into the
childhood he never got to
finish

beauty queens

they come in here everynight
these beauty queens
twenty or thirty years past their prime
their once tight and tanned skin
now faded to wrinkled masses
of liver spots and scars
trying to hide the abuse and anguish
behind caked on make up

they come in here everynight
looking for free drinks
a bed to fuck in
and a wallet to steal from

they come in here everynight
searching for a fool

and when they come in here
i finish my drink
pay my bill
and leave

i figure this fool
better get going
while there's
still a chance

birthdays

just
another
day to
celebrate

getting
one step
closer

to
becoming
irrelevant

boyish good looks

dancing with death
as i pretend these
watercolors are
actually helping

i'm old enough now
to be comfortable
with it

the evil that persists
inside me

not all of us get
to be the hero

besides

i've lost any boyish
good looks it would
take to pull off that
role

and thank god

for the years it has
taken to grow this
goatee

i might as well be
some evil overlord
in the latest sci-fi
piece of shit coming
to a theater near you

burning bridges

i remember when i was younger
my mother told me

never to burn any bridges
for you never know

when you might need something
from that person

in the future
but as i grew older

i realized that
some people aren't worth

building a fucking
bridge for

and that it's better
to burn them

before they get the chance
to burn you

child like innocence

a shock to the system

a punch to the gut

the endless pain of
questions
answers too raw to
be consumed

feeling numb

not even the morning
cocktail can do the trick
anymore

but if it wasn't for the
routines

wake shit eat work pray
cry sleep church guilt

questioning a god that
you can no longer view
with child like innocence

would be so much harder
to confront on this never
ending trail

this quest
this suspension of belief

in hope to one day stumble
upon the truth

love

a child's embrace

a lover's glance

happiness and peace wrapped
in something that doesn't leave
a bad taste in your mouth

a suffering that brings a
nirvana that the wingless
angels can comfort you in

chocolate cake for breakfast

i realized today that i no
longer have the capacity
to give a shit about anything

i stumbled upon this realization
while slicing myself a piece
of chocolate cake for breakfast

and while eating it slowly
savoring each bite

the phone was ringing
the cats were in need of water
and there was plenty of snow
to be shoveled

yet i was pretending i was nero
marching to my own drummer
as reality crumbles around me

i'll gladly waste me time choking
on the dreams of high stakes poker
games in vegas and all the hot
moms i'd like to fuck,
i thought to myself as my fork scraped
up the crumbs from the plate

eventually, i did pick up the
phone though

old habits die hard

but i'm pretty sure that telemarketer
would have preferred to get the machine

for i imagine his ear is still
ringing from the wrath of my
newborn decadence

classical music

i've been
listening
to a lot of
classical
music
lately

i've always
thought
anyone
in their 30's
that listens
to classical
music is
either
pretentious
or a fucking
psychopath

and to tell
the truth

i've always
wanted to
be a little
of both

columbus day

    i
    thought
    i
    would
    spend
    this
    stupid
    holiday
    the
    way
    columbus
    would
    have
    but
    i
    didn't
    think
    the
    cops
    would
    get
    the
    point
    of
    me
    burning
    down
    the
    village
    and
    giving
    everyone
    a
    sexually
    transmitted
    disease

convict pussy

i haven't got the
look from a woman
in many years now

not the what the fuck
are you looking at get
away look mind you

but the well look at that
how you doin' look

so when i got an email the
other day from one of the
few women ever to give
me the look

i quickly dialed the
number she sent me

she went on to tell me
how she just got out
from a year in prison

is now living in a
halfway house of
sorts

and is truly in desire of
some dick

the desire turned to
begging as she explained
she was only an hour away
could give me gas money
etc. etc.

and i thought to myself

this is what my life has
come to

convict pussy

i grabbed my keys
and headed for the
door

dangling from the rooftops again

another night the gun tastes
sweeter than this whore's tongue

dangling from the roof tops again
hoping the rope will snap

because you have realized
that the only reason you were born
was to serve

from god to country
to parents to spouse
to employer to time

and that nasty feeling deep
in your stomach is the
last bit of life
they have force fed you

and when you pull that trigger
you know that all
of this is meaningless

that you were never meant
to serve anyone

not even yourself

discarded

here i go again

rummaging through these random words
hoping to find brilliance on the
discarded napkins of our lives

death
 despair
pain
 agony

the impending demise of my fellow man

i'm pretty certain insanity lurks in
my next cup of coffee
but i don't mind

i've faced the same fucking
odds since conception

with all these years waiting for
the other shoe to drop
you can't help but to eventually
take it for granted

and to tell you the truth

i'll actually be happy
when insanity does arrive

then maybe all of this
will make some fucking
sense for once

the voices and outbursts

the urge in the middle of the night to
kill the baby and start a rampage

that would make prisoners blush

and what explanation could there be
for all these jackie collins books

fuck, i hope i am insane

for i'm too fat, hairy and lack
the flexibility to be gay

i'm busy playing with matches again

something about that
lingering scent just
drives me wild

did you know that
the pages of the bible
burn better than these
cheaply printed books?

but i don't care for the smell
of fleeting control

you would think i'd be due
for some catharsis
but my knees are old
too old to kneel anymore

i learned a long time ago
to never fear the unknown
rather
embrace it like money from
a stranger

fuck

finally the napkin i was looking for

should have known i guess
i never do get these damn numbers
right anymore

i suppose i'm over-educated
to win the lottery

plus, i still have
all of my teeth

good thing i believe in patience
and have many years of good
drinking ahead of me

down in a hole

she went by the name of jaguar

i remember she had a small tattoo
of the playboy bunny on her
right inner thigh

her favorite song was "down in a hole"
by alice in chains, which, given the
position of that bunny
i found quite humorous

i would jerk off to jag
every morning for months it
seemed in some
peep show chat room

i haven't seen her online in
quite some time

but i wake up each morning
knowing that bunny got
closer than i ever did

of course, the bunny was
never asked to pay
$2.19 a fucking minute
either

driving

driving out here in the country
on these old back roads
everyone drives too fast
but as usual
you have a few sunday drivers

and they are always
followed by impatient teens
running late for some
shit job they hate or thinking
about how they would love
to fuck the girl next to them
in history class without
the girlfriend finding out

they always pass the sunday drivers
on blind curves or coming
down these steep hills

and it's always me in the other lane
smoking a cigarette
listening to the radio
watching these fools drive

and it doesn't scare me
when i see them getting closer
i actually hit the gas
wanting to show these kids
what reality is all about

and as they swerve back over
to avoid the inevitable

they look to see me laughing
blowing them a kiss
hoping they have some
clean underwear in the glovebox

for fear really does stink
and it has a tendency
to cling to the body
for extended periods of time

ellen barkin

i've always wanted
to fuck ellen barkin

there's just something
about her that has always
driven me crazy

overwhelmed me with
a sensation of hoping
to bump into her one
night and go fuck her
behind a dumpster
in a dark alley

but sadly, as the years
have gone by and i have
moved further and further
down the food chain of life

i realize my chances
of fucking ellen barkin
are slim and none

so i look for aspects
of her in other women

the hairstyle, the eyes,
the body type, the pantsuits,
the first or last name,

that certain look while
wearing sunglasses indoors

maybe a friend of a friend
of a friend who lost a bet to
the gardener of a friend of a
friend whose son stole her
panties from the trash

i don't know about that
one but i'm doing my best
to keep hope alive

envy

        sitting in my easy chair
        naked
        listening to mozart
        stroking my penis

        out of the corner
        of my eye
        i see my cat
        licking her ass

        i get out of my chair
        turn the music off
        put my clothes back on

        envy
        has ruined
        my good time

even hell and back

your hatred is a
beautiful light
that blinds me
every time i fall
to my knees

i always wanted
my love to win
this war

and as i lay here

another night

alone

i realize losing
is one sour fucking
taste that is hard
to get rid of

no matter the
lengths one is
willing to travel
to

fleeting at best

i lack the proper motivation
for a man my age

the reckless abandon of my youth
left me years ago

i lost my sense of
urgency along the way

any notion of desire, passion, ambition
or drive is fleeting at best

my family and friends wonder why
it's come to this

they plead with me to seek help

beg for me to find god, the bottle,
take up a hobby and keep
the guns locked away

they don't believe me
when i tell them i'm fine
i am perfectly at ease with
my lot in life, these cards
suit me just fine

their concerns persist as the
experts explain to them
that the end could be drawing near

figures

i was just starting to
enjoy myself

from my empty bed

someone once told me
if i learned how to dance
i would always have
a woman by my side

and as i write this
from my empty bed

i realize that was one
piece of advice i should
have actually listened to

games

she likes to make me angry

tells me i fuck her
better that way

i laugh

tell her that's not anger
fucking her better

that's my imagination of
someone other than her

she fucks better angry as well

hatred

this woman asked me once
how does one so young
get to be so old

i told her it's hard work
but i recommend living alone
listening to the music
of great dead men
and never seek out the crowds

for if you are genius
they will find you
no matter which rock
you try to hide under

and when they find you
they will eventually grow to
hate you

which is for the best
i tell her

for love has
all kinds of peaks and valleys

but hatred
on the otherhand

hatred is definite

like a bullet in the back of the head
like a knife to the gut
like death tapping you on the shoulder

love comes and goes as she pleases

but hatred
hatred shall always be there

homeless

they're pissing in the park again
because the library is charging admission
to visit the porcelain god
but they're happy they have a park to piss in
and i watch them sit there
with their last cigarette and paper bag bottle of wine
wondering if the yuppies
are going to spare fifty cents today
spontaneous charity is a rarity
they're much more appreciative
of a smile
of a handshake
some warm talk to ease the lingering madness
of a cold snowy day
but as they pray to the statue
with no eyes
they realize that no movie script day
will ever come to them
they are only holding on to life
until they find it necessary
to succumb to death

hoping this tension will bring the truth

you could cut the tension between us
with the same knife you've threatened
to run across your wrists for years now

with each touch of your lips
i could taste the blood that
will connect us forever

and whether we wanted it,
needed it, or even cared that the
moment had arrived
it was over now

much like when boys throw rocks
at the stained glass windows of a church
when that glass shatters, do you run
and hide or do you confess?

we're at that crossroad now

stumbling over the empty boxes of wine
and ashtrays overflowing with
the remnants of drunken intellectuals

i imagine this is as good a time
as any to start the killing spree

but we both know we can't trust
anyone who bleeds better than the
warrior in our souls

so, like any struggle of good
and evil, it is that lonely path
that we both must ride

hoping that our faith
brings us truth

for i don't think either of us
seek salvation

just the truth to
bring this journey
to an end will suffice

i have the scars to prove it

i made the mistake once
when i was younger
of telling a joke
when this woman
was giving me
a blowjob

it was on that day
that i discovered
the first rule of comedy
really is
timing

i woke up this morning

and realized
i'm an alcoholic
there's something about
waking up in a
pile of your own shit
that makes things
pretty fucking clear

i hate my father

father's day passed
this year without a
i hate my father
poem

and i don't know
if it's i'm maturing

or time has healed
old wounds

or perhaps it's i
have finally got it
through my thick
skull that none of
this fucking
matters

here's life

it sucks

move on

i like mom better anyway

i've practiced the conversation
about a thousand times

just in case she doesn't want
an abortion

just in case a swift kick down a
couple flights of stairs doesn't
do the trick

just in case hush money isn't
accepted

i've practiced the conversation
explaining to my child why i'm
inadequate as a father nearly a
thousand times

starting off about how my father
never told me he loved me unless
my mother forced him to

how my father never showed me
how to build or fix anything
helping was either holding a ladder
or staying the fuck out of the way

how my father never showed me
how to interact in public without
being loaded on alcohol

how my father… and it's at this
point where my child stops me
and says i get it dad, you're an
asshole, it's ok, i like mom
better anyway

that's much better than how my last
conversation went with my father

i told him if he threatened my
mother again, i'd kill him

of course, i'm prepared for the
threat of death from my child

after all

given the history of this gene pool
it seems the only natural way

idle thoughts on a sunday night

listening to billie holiday

watching this woman
get fucked over by the
pool on tv

occasionally drinking from
this bottle of beer

wondering if the money shot
will come before i
finish this poem

guess not

in the local section

i read in the
newspaper
this morning
a 14 year old
boy is accused
of raping a 64
year old woman

i tell ya

these kids grow
up so damn fast
these days

in the valley of this connected generation

dancing with
the demons that
brought me

making my way
through dying
insects and burning
bible verses

i want to go
swimming in
a river and see
where it takes me

i know your love
is on the other side

somewhere in
the valley of this
connected generation

we're only a 24/7
news cycle from
our last goodbye

lips laced with
bourbon and the
music makes me
believe this might
have a chance

of course
alcohol had a way
with clarity that i
never did

an endless
desperation

stuck on a
crumbling
tower

our death only a
few smiles away

irony

it
could
have
been
nothing
but
complete
irony
when
i
called
my
ex
girlfriend
yesterday
we
exchanged
the
obligatory
small
talk
bullshit
and
so
forth
all
the
while
she
was
sitting
on
the
toilet
taking
a
piss

junkies of death

fading screams

lost in the shallow
flickers of light
creeping through
a thick fog

we were great at
this

this being whatever
you need this to be

frustration mounts

the words don't
seem to fit

broken glass
ripped up pages

broken egos scattered
on an old dusty floor

sweep them up with
the rest of the filth

trash will be picked
up tomorrow

the rightful resting
place for all of us

us being this collective
mass of bullshit artists,
con men, junkies of
death

hoping to escape the
consequences of time

just another sweaty fat fuck

"i bet you look sexy," she said
"out there mowing the grass, sunglasses
on, sun reflecting off your skin…"

i just let her keep going

figure i'll save the
disappointment for
when we meet

then she'll realize that i'm
just another sweaty fat fuck

the kind of guy you see
working in the yard as
you're driving by that just
makes you want to
pull over and scream

FOR THE LOVE OF GOD
PUT ON A FUCKING SHIRT

kung fu theater of the mind

each time i look
into your eyes it's
like i am stuck in
the kung fu theater
of the mind

those lovely curves
and my eager hands
always seem to be
one step out of sync

and this constant
miscommunication
has this poor boy
seeing blue

though i learned a
long time ago

never leave a kung
fu movie before the
end

nudity always happens
when you least expect
it

like a fading kiss

a lilywhite nirvana
of broken mattresses
and slide trombones

she had the eyes
of the ancient
dead greeks

i didn't stare long
enough to turn to
stone

she asked for more
salsa at this trendy
cinco de mayo tent
party

i asked for more
lightning, maybe
a tornado and a
quick exit

failure

like a fading kiss
on a wet spring
night

to be rubbed out
in the next thirty
seconds of the
home shopping
network

who knew that
color would look
good on the
thick girl

like it nearly had a meaning

i could see it in your
eyes

those deep dark pools
of regret
remorse
unrequited love

winter was settling in

the winds bringing the
harsh chill of death to
your door

be it an unwanted
child

a pet left to die outside
in the snow

or an old mother left to
fade in nursing home
madness

it was written in a pale
sky

your last breath hung in
the air like it nearly had
a meaning

a purpose

a reason to exist in the
first place

the clouds shall part and
all will be forgiven and

washed away

folded neatly into a back
pocket

to be forgotten forever

living in my stereo(type)

i'm a living, breathing,
walking stereotype

white male, late twenties,
unemployed

i live with my mother

i write poems and
masturbate the day away

i'm not that far
away from fulfilling
that stereotype

i think i may be a few
steps closer actually
now that i have moved all
my shit into the basement

soon, i'm hoping to seal the deal
by getting that longed for
pizza delivery job to cover
for my budding career
as a minor dope dealer

just a few heat lamps away
from my white trash utopia

making a list, checking it twice

i'm wearing my sunglasses in
a thunderstorm again

dreaming about the days when
i wanted to grow up and be the politician
who refused to kiss the ugly babies

while drinking my body weight
in southern comfort each day

the grocery store kind though
life is a marathon, not a sprint

back when i thought that all my
freckles would join together one day
and make a glorious permanent tan

that was nothing more than another
installment in my long history of failure

you would think it would end
somewhere but no,
that's what i get for thinking

time to put the brain aside
and listen to the gut

of course

the gut has been nagging at me for
years to turn this pen into a gun
these words into bullets and this sheet
of paper into a place for
collecting names

i still say i'd be
better off as a poet

but who am i to
question
my
calling

mission accomplished

sometimes i sit in
my room all day
just listening to
music

maybe penning a
poem or two

thinking about
painting

thumbing through
some old books

strumming a
guitar

then popping in
an old porno

i remember when
i was 13 i never
wanted to grow
up

now in my mid
30's

molly ringwald

sitting here listening to cheap trick
while going through the dreaded
box of high school memories

the smell of incense is still in the air

i close my eyes and wonder

when the fuck did my life
become a fucking john hughes movie?

i suppose it was well before
this box was ever full

but the more important question is

where the fuck is my molly ringwald?

i mean shit, i've played the
lovable loser long enough
to merit the happy fucking
ending by now

right?

hello?

molly?

hopefully some kind soul
will roll the end credits
on this fucker shortly

my ball of energy

here i am again
draining my bloody tears
into another bottle of truth
as i struggle to cope with
the fruits of my bitter
existence

but i notice as that war rages on
other things come with ease now

such as the bullet finding
the chamber

no more guilt

no more fear

the trembles of anxiety
become my ball of energy
piercing deep into the core
of another stormy night

as for where the bullet ends up
your guess is as good as mine

i don't bother to check
the names anymore

i leave that to god

my father's sentiments on my 18th birthday

i read somewhere once
that the happiest day
in a man's life
is when his child is born
if that's the case
then i guess
the second happiest day
is when he's
no longer forced
to pay child support

my life in a black high school

hopeless

a drowning
pool of guilt

it's obvious
to me

i was never
meant to swim
upstream

my luck with the ladies

i remember that night i took
you to the drive-in

we parked off to the side
so not to be disturbed

and right when we started
to make out
i started to feel sick

not sick from kissing you

but sick to my stomach
probably from something i ate

and then it hit me
that oh shit, i got to go
explosion in the brain

i made my mad dash
walking as fast as i could while
squeezing the cheeks of my ass tight

a few feet from the bathroom
some evil force ripped my ass cheeks
apart and suddenly a massive amount
of hot brown poo was filling my shorts

i made it into the stall and ripped my
shorts down and just stared at the mess

"seventeen years old and i'm shitting on
myself like i'm eighty," i thought

i stayed in there for damn near
thirty minutes, cleaning myself
and my clothes off

i got most of it but the stench
was unbearable

i walked back to the car
head lowered in embarrassment

i explained to you that i had an accident
and had to leave

you were very understanding and said
that you had some friends there that
you could catch a ride with

i thought it was rather nice of you
to wait until i left to bust out laughing
which i imagine you did, or perhaps
i'm just paranoid

anyways, i drove home

went right upstairs and got in the shower

i cried in the shower that night
cried like a little baby

that was over ten years ago now

my luck with the ladies
hasn't changed much

if at all

my personal pam grier

i spent the majority of
black history month
jerking off to black
women online, hoping
to find my personal
pam grier

all i ever got though
other than the occasional
slip of a nipple or a flash
of pussy was raw and bored

one of which doesn't
remind me of pam grier

but does remind me
of the countless black
girls i tried to date back
in high school

thankfully i have aged
since then and the years
gone by seem to have
a way of putting the past
many miles behind

and thank god that
boredom never became
a pregnancy

for i've got a good clue
what my child would be
doing in future black
history months

wanna go private baby,
only $1.99 a minute

nothing but the dog in me

sitting here naked
drunk
smoking a cigarette
listening to miles davis
i can feel
the animal in me
coming alive

maybe that's why
i was rubbing
my dirty ass
on the carpet

now i believe

a 62 foot high
statue of jesus
burned to the
ground after a
lightning strike

all the while the
hustler megastore
across the highway
was left untouched
by the storm

now i believe
in god

on my porch

i like to sit on my porch
with a beer and a cigar
and watch the young girls walk by

with their hot short skirts
and long tan legs
tight shirts meant to accentuate
still forming breasts
their hair is always glowing
and they have that special wiggle
in their ass

they never turn to look at me
becoming aroused
licking my lips
thinking of what i could do

they've been warned
about dirty old men on porches

but the fat ones
the ugly ones
the virgins that sit in school
all day long and listen
to the sexual exploits of their friends

they always turn and smile

they know their reality

you've got to take
what you can get

it's my reality as well

on the curve of your hips

dark steamy
eyes

sultry lips

time fucking
stops on the
curve of your
hips

no need to kid
ourselves

neither one of
us are looking
for love

maybe a few
drinks

time will pass

inhibition
hopefully
will follow

long before you
come

to your senses

one for isabella

another rainy
afternoon

just me and the
anal sex toys

colombian women

a little social d in
the background

and a shitty dial-up
internet connection

they say patience
is a virtue

but so is plenty of
available credit

the flexible ones
always cost more

only your imagination

it's that awkward
feeling when you
believed a beautiful
woman was staring
at you only to realize
it was only your
imagination fucking
around

it's feeling alone in
a crowded room

sleeping with one
eye open

keeping a gun and
a bottle nearby

but even you have
realized there's no
magic tricks left in
them

and the problem
being a one trick
pony is when you're
the last to know

lock the doors and
hide under the covers

read up and be sure

no one wants to
survive the final
shot

our hero tattooed in black lace

the shock of the news will
hit me hard given my love
and adoration for you

the overwhelming silence will
climb on top of me like a lover
from many years ago

the funeral home will be packed

i will be the one they are
shocked to see

i'll bypass the long line of well
wishers and head straight to your
modest, but not cheap looking,
casket

i will slip you some heroin to help
you on your journey and whisper
into your ear

death never looked as beautiful
as it does on you

i'll kiss your forehead and slip
out the side door

satisfied in knowing that this
was the only ending that would
suit either one of us

but nothing will ever replace
the space, the face, the punk
rock grace, the new wave taste
of our hero tattooed in black lace

the demons will never chase

you again but your words will
haunt each and every one of us

just as they should

paralyze

i still think about the way
you would touch me

the electricity that would run
up and down my spine

i'd be paralyzed with anticipation
and you never disappointed

it's on these nights alone
with the frigid winter air

empty bottles scattered around
pacing these floors

counting my steps as i slowly
descend into madness

that i can't help but wonder
who are you paralyzing now

patiently waiting at the station

i recently had this back wood
conservative christian fuck
(not that there's anything wrong with that)
from mississippi read my poetry
and tell me i needed god in my life

when my answers to his questions
didn't quench his thirst to
pass judgment on me
he told me he would contact the
proper authorities and tell them
i'm a pedophile

i told him he had to do
what he had to do
but there was no need for him to worry

for i am many miles away
and his children would be
fucked up long before i got there
given the fact that he and
the state in which he resides in
are both having problems coming
to terms with the 21st century

at least that's my thinking
behind the reason why
he hasn't reported me yet

and how i yearn for him to be
a man of more than just words
so that train of publicity
can heat up the tracks

performance anxiety

she told me she wanted
my cum all over her face

that was the first time in
my 28 years that an actual
woman and not a video said
those words to me

and in my excitement
i completely missed her face
and shot it all over
the antiques behind her

i guess kissing isn't the
only thing i do with
my eyes closed

pleasure often brings pain

kissing your lips was like
running razor blades
over my wrists

little bits of glass are still
embedded deep in my skin

much like the taste of your
soul is forever branded
upon my memory

i often run the endless questions of
could, should and would
through my mind
when it comes to you

but i always come to the
same conclusion

one suicide was enough
for each of us

priorities

a fuck friend of mine
dropped by the other day
without calling of course

i was in the middle of
watching my favorite
hockey team battle for
a playoff position

when she walked in the door
she found me in my chair
watching the game

she started kissing on me
nibbling on my ear
but i ignored her
then she started to strip

for me
but i ignored her still
then at a commercial break

i looked at her and kissed her
i picked her up
and took her over to
the clothes dryer

i kissed her deep and set
the timer for one hour
then i turned the damn thing on

i went and got a beer
looked back at her and said
when the buzzer goes off,
smoke a cigarette and leave

i went back to my chair
to watch the game

soon i heard the front door

being slammed violently
then a car raced down my lane
gravel went flying
but shit

it was still early in the
second period
and the outcome was in doubt

ramblings of a long winded ass clown

i'm one of them scratch
ass sniff finger types

the gut hanging over the belt
fuck tucking the shirt in kind of
guy that every parent hopes and
prays their son doesn't turn into

i'm controlled by apathy

controlled to the point where bathing
everyday is damn near impossible

but i do think highly enough of myself
that i make sure my sweatpants match the
shirt i'm wearing that day

my apathy has me wondering if i cut my
eyes enough, would they scab over to
the point where they could never open again?

meaningless question actually since i
don't have the patience or the
stomach for such an act

self-mutilation by drink is much more my style

and through this liquid courage
this truth serum, i can tell my
life is coming to a head soon

a war is raging and one battle is left
winner takes all

good vs. evil, right vs. wrong,
night vs. day, yankees vs. red sox

i have money on each side because i'm

a pussy when i bet
but i honestly don't care who wins

for i know the victor doesn't care for the spoils
260 lbs. of flesh and body hair
dry wit and a devious sense of humor
my better days are behind me

of course, that could just be the alcohol talking

for i still wake up each morning
i still take the time to wipe off the cum each day
i still wait at the post office for the lost letters
of love to finally arrive in the mail

there's a hopeless romantic trapped inside
of this fat insane fuck before you

i'm not exactly sure how you found him
but it's not like i really care either

i'm just glad you bothered to fucking look
and weren't put off by the fading paint
on my evil facade

perhaps, i can buy you a drink
get you to stay awhile
talk me down from this ever-present ledge

yes, yes, i know
i'm not going to fucking jump

but can't anyone just take it
seriously for once

i would take off my black sheep clothes
and reveal the wolf inside if i honestly
thought it would make a difference

but i have noticed that apathy
is much like a disease

it spreads at a very high rate
when not taken care of immediately

and to think my high school teachers
thought i wasn't going to use my gifts
the way they were intended to be used

fools, nothing more
than damn fools

sadness, through male eyes

i was going through a
drawer in my desk tonight
and came across some
condoms well past
their expiration date

and here they told me i
would outgrow all those

high school feelings i had
of being a loser

safety first

i was stuck behind this car
on my way into town today

nothing out of the ordinary
actually, male driver
female passenger just
taking their sweet ass time

i looked down to change
the radio station i was
listening to

when i looked back up
i only saw one head in
the car in front of me

suddenly that car took
off flying down the road

then i noticed a little swerving
and the brakes being pumped
then the gas floored again

i started to laugh and
figured a little road head
was going on in there

i stayed back, didn't want to
get caught up in a potentially
embarrassing car accident

but i did get a good chuckle
when i noticed the driver
had his seat belt on

in the back of my mind
i could hear one of those

old driver's education
tapes being played

safety first is the key to
any enjoyable experience
in a motor vehicle

sara

cowboy boots
a flowing skirt

just enough
leg to rev the
engines of my
imagination

angelic voice

blended in
with the fiddle

the bow of
heartbreak
and desire
all set to the
rhythm of
jimmie rodgers

what i wouldn't
give for twenty
minutes and the
chance that you
wouldn't be
completely
fucking bored
with me

but i can't
help but think
i would simply
become a creepy
character for your
next song

saving the world from a future ungrateful bastard

a woman asked me tonight
if she could borrow my
sperm one day to have a
child that i would never
have to have anything
to do with

i politely declined, citing
my belief that my father's
dna shouldn't pollute the
earth any longer than it
absolutely has to

she understood my
reasoning given her
own dysfunctional
upbringing

but she reiterated that i
was the only man that
she would ever want
to father her child

i told her thanks as
the names and faces
of countless other
men better suited for
the job ran through
my head

she did say i was cute though

this older woman sent
me an instant message
the other day

she read some of my
poetry and thought it was
really good

and she just happens to live
in the same town as i do
as well

so naturally,
the conversation soon turned to
sex (imagine that) and before
too long

she agreed to come over
and fuck away the rest of the
dreary day

she signed off to go shower
and i signed off and waited

and waited

and waited

waited long enough to realize
maybe my poetry isn't that
good after all

she did say i was cute though

a small victory
but, alas

another battle lost

she refused to drink it

i watched
a woman
take a piss
in a video
chat room
while my
mother was
in the next
room

i think i
finally
found
how a
loser in
his thirties
finds joy

social anxiety disorder

so there i was in some trendy
save the downtown industrial
district restaurant for my mother's
fifty-fifth birthday party

surrounded by family and her friends
the kind of shit i normally avoid

and sure enough, after a hour and a
few beers i'm on the toilet

and it's the kind of bloody shit that
for as much shit that makes the toilet
there is an equal amount on the floor
and in your pants

the kind of shit that you know
you'll never be able to wipe it all

the kind of shit bukowski made
famous

and like clockwork, back out at the
table i could feel the stink start to
fester up my spine

and looking over at all the young hot
barmaids and waitresses i could feel
the depression getting ready to set up
camp

it was right about then that the cousin
that molested me as a child handed me
a piece of cake

i could hear god laughing over in the
corner with all the cool kids

and as i got up to leave and noticed the
little bit of blood and shit on the chair

i reminded myself that on days like these
men much better than me have killed
themselves

i can only wonder what i'm waiting for

sometimes i wish i was pink

sometimes when i'm shaving
i'll completely lose myself
in various thoughts

and this one time i was
in my own version of
pink floyd's the wall

so there i was shaving
this one spot on my face
over and over and over again
until there was nothing but blood
and it slowly rolled down my
face and into the sink
drop by drop

then i started to focus
on my eyebrows
wonder what i would
look like without them

but i quickly tossed that
thought aside
thinking that without eyebrows
my chances of getting pussy
would be even less than they are now

and then in walks my mother
who stares at me

then, with her god awful
english/irish/scottish/
the whole bunch of bloody fucking cunts sound the same
accent
she asks me

what the fuck are ye doin'?

i look at her out of
the corner of my eye
tell her
it's a bloodlettin' ma,
just lettin' the evil spirits out

she turns around shaking her head
partly because she thinks i'm full of shite
and partly because it makes
perfect bloody sense to her

she closes the door
and i go back to looking
at myself in the mirror

the blood is coming off my face
in larger drops now

i look down to see the water
has gone from a
shaving cream white
to this punk pink

that is ever so slightly
beginning to stain the sink

i look up, start to laugh
and think

this is why they keep
the sharp instruments away
from crazy people

sour milk on fruit loops

trying to manufacture
joy on a cloudy day

my body filled to
the brim with pain

squinting my left
eye to see if i can
make out a cloud
of clowns murdering
little children

staring off into
the distance

dead coyotes

grass over a foot tall

and i'm stuck hoping
for the ghosts of dead
farmers to come back
and save something or
someone worthy of
such horseshit

i don't bother to search
for those souls don't
exist anymore

i never thought death
would taste like this

stink

it never fails me

each morning i wake up
i have this nasty shit to take

you know, one of those
where no matter how long
or how much you wipe
you're never quite sure
you got it all

and with time being
of the essence
a shower is out of the question

and of course
it's the summer

90 degrees plus every damn day

so when that first
bead of sweat starts to
roll down my back
i look around me

wonder how long i can fool
these fuckers into thinking
that what they smell
is actually a nearby farm

and not the raging inferno of stink
that is brewing down
here in my jeans

strike up the band

a sense of urgency is
clenched tightly in my hand

blood has started to crawl
from the corner of my mouth

i think i have just realized
that i don't belong here
nor do i believe i ever did

reload the chamber

strike up the band

my last glass of alcohol
shall be my finest

i'll dance these steps
until i get it right

a death worthy
of your love

stuck here in the cold silence

i always wanted to be
one of those smooth motherfuckers

one of those five o'clock shadow guys
that looks good in sunglasses
and a t-shirt

one of those guys who stands in
front of a woman with a long stem rose
and a smile and suddenly every time
you fucked her over is forgiven with only
a little wink and a kiss of the hand

instead

i'm the funny fat ass
with the bushy beard that screams
single white male who lives with
his mother or in his car

the loneliness written all over
my face is my calling card

most women see it as a welcome mat
a place to wipe their feet
take advantage of their time
and move on

hopefully long before the
wrong intentions get mentioned

before they're unable to be brought back
from that cold silence of
i don't look at you in that way
sorry

suicide watch

i often think of the
nights i buried my
face between your
legs

the nights where the
tequila became so
vicious a suicide
watch would be
issued

the nights of unbridled
passion meant for
someone else
someone better

someone
anyone
other than
you and me

the nights of broken glass
and holes in walls shaped
like frustrated fists

the nights where classical
music dripped between
kisses and the moonlight
shadows of pale white walls

the nights where insanity
and utopia created an
invisible line undaunted
by any nose around

this chapter was to end
differently yet somehow

we both made it out alive

i'm sure most wish we
would have stuck to the
original plan

but no script is complete
without a thorough re-write

the american dream

i remember being in class one day
and the teacher asked us all
what our definition
of the american dream was

everyone talked about the spouse,
kids, a fireplace, the white picket fence,
the two car garage, the nice job, and nice car

then it got to me and i told
my fellow classmates that they
were all fucking stupid

the american dream
is coming home everyday
without a pink slip in your hand
or a bullet in your back

with that there was silence
everyone glared at me
they didn't like me
i always had to bring reality into it

i chose not to have any delusions about
my future and they hated me for it

and here it is
nearly five years later
and i live out my
american dream everyday (so far)

while the rest of them in that class
are either dead, in jail, or busy
toiling away, sold on the belief
that one day their american dream will come true

in the meantime
i light up a cigarette

and crack open a beer
glad to know that i have
no desire to be somebody

the bitch with the black eye

watching the local
evening news when
a woman with a
black eye comes
on and talks about
a hit and run accident
on her street

i said that must be on
the east side of town

and my sister looks
up and says hold up,
ain't no one gonna
say shit about the
bitch with the black
eye

and i laughed, said
it's pretty obvious
she only had to be
told once

and my mother
laughed

it's good to know
where i get my
sick sense of
humor from

and it's always
good when a
domestic violence
joke brings the
family closer
together

the cruel circle of loneliness

i remember
hearing when
i was younger
that if you had
no one to share
your success
with those
successes really
didn't mean
much

and thirty five
years into this
experience that's
the fucking truth

yet i'm still here

just fucking
stubborn enough
to prove them
wrong

one painful day
at a time

though i suppose
when i do prove
them wrong

i'll be the only
one to know

the enigma

i am the underbelly of
democracy
capitalism
apple pie and baseball
and all those other things
we were taught to be truth
the only truth

i am the broken home child
with unlimited knowledge
but instead of going to college
and having to pay the government back
until i'm forty
i'm working
writing shitty poems
masturbating six times a day
to cable tv

i am the quiet one
the next door neighbor
that will commit suicide
or molest children
or be a serial killer

i am the one the media
will pay no attention to
until i do wrong
for i'm middle class
i'm not a minority
just a bored
fucked up human
and the media doesn't pay
attention to those
nor do i believe they should

i am the enigma
that people will try
to figure out

and then quit
give up
move on to other things
that their brains
don't have to work at

i am the relative
you hear rumors about
but never see
or even think to remember
when the holidays come around

i am the one
in the back of the class
plotting
my
revenge

the outskirts of downtown

a crack whore gave me
and a buddy a striptease
in my living room a few
years back

now i didn't know she
was a crack whore until
i was driving her home
at seven in the morning

she pleaded for me to
drive her to a certain place
to buy a rock

after a few moments of
hesitation i decided to say
yes as a little voice inside
of me yelled to be a good
writer you need shit to
write about

so i pulled into these
projects on the outskirts
of downtown

there were four black guys
about a quarter mile down
the road selling behind an
apartment building

as i pulled up i pointed to
the passenger side so they
would know who was
interested in buying

as she negotiated a deal
one of the black guys

came around to my side
of the car

my window was down as
it was a very hot morning
as i remember

he pointed his gun in
the car and said you
betta put this car in
park or i'm gonna blow
your fucking brains out

i chuckled and slipped the
car into park as a bit of piss
started to run down my leg

she bought a small rock for
ten dollars which i didn't
think was the best deal she
could have made but i was
in no position or mood to
argue my point

after my nuts dropped to
their normal position i put
the car in drive and headed
to her home

a nice three story
upper middle class place
in the suburbs

she wrote her number down
on a hard pack of marlboro
lights

we said our goodbyes and i

was on my way back to the
farm

i enjoyed the cigarettes but
i never called her

i figured once was enough

besides if she talked me into
taking her to the projects again
i had a feeling that black guy
would stick something other
than a gun near my mouth

the rapture

a freshly planted
field of corn now
under water

tornado warnings

hail the size of
softballs

we all should
have known the
rapture wasn't
going to happen
until oprah's final
show had aired

thunder

lightning

wave after wave
twenty minutes
apart

standing by the
new bay window
watching this old
tree hang on for
dear life

i might as well
pull up a chair
and wait to see
if it starts raining
frogs

the shallow end of the gene pool

i remember when i was younger
and my father told people that he
married my mother because he needed
someone to knock the shit
out of his underwear

i found that funny back then
but as i got older, it slowly dawned
on me that i came from the
shallow end of the gene pool

and no matter how hard i tried
to overcome those odds that were
stacked against me since birth

it always felt like i was just
spinning my wheels, making no
progress at all

so, i've decided to just face facts

i'm in my late twenties
single, no kids, living at home
with my mother

i quit

i no longer am looking for that
"dream" woman
that bundle of beauty and brains who
has the uncanny ability to handle
all my hereditary shit

i now only wish to find a woman
who can give my hands a good
five minute break

which i've found is a

pretty big challenge
due to the fact that out of all
the "gifts" my father bestowed upon me
i guess the gift of a bigger dick was
simply out of the question

the unexpected death of an old friend

i never realized your beauty
until i saw you in your casket

the soft and gentle features
of your face were lost
upon me until then

and perhaps it was that
or maybe just seeing you
finally at peace
that brought these tears

i wiped them with my hand
and pressed my hand to your lips

who would have thought that
out of all the juices we
shared over the years
the ones that meant the most
would come after your death

the urinal for little boys

i always feel a little
weird taking a piss in
a public restroom in
the urinal next to the
urinal for little boys

i always feel like i'm
going to turn around
one day and there's
going to be an officer
with a 6 year old saying
yes sir, there's the guy
that touched me

and the officer wouldn't
think twice about a boy
with an incredible
imagination for i'm
always a little unkempt,
crazy looking

i fit the stereotype
nicely

but i'd rather take the
chance than piss my
pants

so i try to get done as
fast as possible

fighting back the urge
to take a peek

the wheels on the bus go round and round

often on my way home
from work in the morning
I end up behind a school bus

and I begin to fantasize
about some young slut
sitting in the backseat
flashing me her tits
showing some leg
or some panties

but that fantasy
never comes true

it's always some young fucker
crew cut and pimples
giving me the finger

which I simply laugh at
because I know damn well
that I was doing the same thing
when I was their age

especially when some dirty
old fuck was leering in

searching for his next victim

the spark of my youth

i keep listening to the
music of my teenage
years hoping to find
the spark of my youth

but as i wake each
morning and am
greeted at the mirror
with disappointment

i sadly realize those
old tunes are out of
magic

think before speaking

i want to think i have
mellowed since my
teenage years

but my blood still
boils in just a matter
of seconds

the need for conflict
still runs deep

though unlike my
teenage years

i've learned to
count to ten

take a few deep
breaths

think before
speaking

but none of that
means i won't strike
when i smell fear

you don't make it
in my world without
stomping on a few
souls along the way

this lovely mess

there's a faint
trace of blood
and shit in the
air

these old
women trying
to hold onto
youth

yet youth ran
away many
moons ago

and there is
no amount of
make-up, fishnets,
gaping assholes,
or lip injections
that will recapture
it

though, i'm just
lonely enough to
appreciate the
effort

another drink for
this lovely mess
sitting here

this silly episode called life

another freeze warning
in the middle of spring

chopin never sounded
so sad

your eyes haunt me like
the past of a priest

would and should are
out making bets on my
next mistake

it's lonely out here when
your own ego gets tired
of the same shit

but i wouldn't say i'm lost

lost ones have no clue
of the ending

i know my demise rests
in the gun closet down
the hall

and i close my eyes each
night understanding that
some demon inside me has
a fixation on perfect timing
and whenever that fucker
decides to roll film

this silly episode called life
can finally proceed

time has been much kinder to her

and there she was

the first real love of
my life

sitting across from me
in the living room

nearly ten years since
we've seen each other

time has been much
kinder to her

same lovely face
amazing smile
wonderful body
ass for days

and when i find myself
getting lost in her eyes
i revert back to the 16
year old dumbass who
had two left feet and
no clue what a woman
wanted

yet trying to play
the part

my ass cheeks clinched
tightly together doing
my best to hold in a fart

she got a phone call
and i excused myself
to the bathroom

laughing

like holding in a fart
gives me a better chance
at whatever

trash

digging through the trash
any street corner
any big city

they are looking for the america
they read about
the one they saw in the movies
the apple pies
the wealth
the streets full of gold
and names in neon

instead they are rummaging
for french fries
discarded cigarettes
waiting for the better off
to come off a few coins
so that one day
they can buy a meal

but unlike most of us
they haven't quit
they don't think of themselves
as failures
and when they look
in the mirror each day
they don't think about suicide

they just look at it as
another day the
american dream may come true

unlike us
this not as good as the rest
mass of society

we look in the mirror each day
with no hope

no dreams
praying that a random bullet
has our name on it

on it

tuesday afternoon sex

so here we are
two sweat drenched piles of flesh
laying on bloody sheets

disillusioned
frustrated
unsure of the words to come next

i reach for a towel
and my pants
she turns her back to me in bed

how do you tell a woman
that although you don't mind
fucking her the reason you
don't cum with her
is that you're simply
not attracted to her

after thinking about it
i realize there is no way to
tell her if i expect her
to fuck me again

so i tell her i'm sorry
it's not her fault
that i've been
depressed and tired

she looks at me and says
she understands
kisses me on the lips

apparently forgetting that what i
told her was the same thing
i told her six months ago

we both got dressed and i

walked her to her car

we kissed goodbye and she told me
how she will see me
in another couple of months

i said ok, knowing damn well
no matter how much i
want to end it with her

and spare us these unsuccessful forays
into ecstasy

my dick is the head of that department
and he'll have none of that

unemployment

this woman paid
me $10 today
to watch me
masturbate and then
shoot the outcome
of my efforts
into her mouth
when i was done

let's just say
this whole
unemployment
thing may work
out for me after all

untitled grief on a september afternoon

found out this
morning that
jim carroll
died

heart attack
they say

another damn
episode of my
youth fades
to black

rest in peace

you truly
deserve
it

up by the big barn

there are a couple of guys
(think deliverance and a banjo)
that like to come out here
and hunt coyotes

just for fun as one guy put it

so no later than three minutes
of them coming up the lane
and parking their truck
three shots were fired and there
was a knock at the door

do you wanna see it?

the yankees just got swept
i've got a stack of rejection
letters and my fantasy baseball
teams have gone to shit

of course i want to see it

it was of medium size
bright red blood still flowing

they shot it up by the big barn
the one my cat has taken a
liking to visit each day

some people find a certain
beauty in dead animals
either in deep reflection
or in venomous anger

i'm not one of those

this was a nuisance snuffed
good riddance

the guys left with the dead
coyote in the back of the truck
off to do with it what they wish

hat
stew

they look like the useful kind

welcome to the small press kid

they are counting on
my demise just as much
as i am

somehow i feel we will
both come up on the
short end of that stick

leave it to me

just apathetic enough
that it seems fucking
cool

losers my friend

we are nothing
but losers

rearranging the thoughts
and words of the better
losers that came before
us

what is rain

i
remember
when
i
was
younger
i
asked
my
parents
what
is
rain
and
they
told
me
that
it's
god
crying

yeah
i'd
cry
too
if
they
were
holding
me
responsible
for
this
fucking
mess

while masturbating today

after years of fantasizing
about shooting my load
on some hot woman's face
watching her lick her lips
her cheeks glistening
sperm dripping off her chin
like spring water coming
down a mountain

it figures
the first face
i would
shoot it on
would be my own

wish you were here

i remember it quite well

we were both in our teens

downstairs in the basement
holding each other on the couch

pink floyd's "wish you were here"
came on the radio

we both started to sing along

i'm pretty sure we were both
singing to different people
but that never changed the strength
and warmth of our embrace

a surreal moment to say the least

it was the first moment i had
with a member of the opposite sex
that didn't involve animal
magnetism or the words
"i love you like a brother"

that was damn near twenty
years ago now

i haven't had many of those
types of moments since

and the more i dwell on it

the harder it is for me to think that
someone could feel emptier
than i do right now

wishful thinking

so there i was last night
talking to this sexy woman on the phone
and she's telling me how her dog
is right between her legs
how she's petting it and
giving it kisses

and if there ever was a time in my life
that i wished the superhero powers
i thought i had as a child
were actually true
this was the one

so i closed my eyes
thought really hard
clicked my heels three times
said some magic words
anything trying to become that dog

after 10 minutes
i opened my eyes to find me
in my chair, naked and aroused
but still unable to lick my balls

and that's why i hate my childhood
the lie of my mother telling me
that if i put my mind to it
i can do anything

with no peaceful resolution in sight

trailer park

small white town
in ohio

a bullet goes
through a trailer

the police are
called

a deputy investigating
the complaint pulls out
her camera to take a
photo of a footprint

that deputy is
shot in the face

a shootout ensues
with her dead body
caught in the middle

another officer is
hit

swat is called

hours pass with
no peaceful resolution
in sight

gunfire erupts

all caught on
video

suspect is dead

either by his
own hand or
swat

no one really
cares at this
point

happy new year

withdrawn

bloody hands
wrapped around what i thought
was the future
dreams/love/forever
it was only another fantasy
turned into a slit wrist night
of loneliness
heartbreak
the tragedy of balcony alcohol
too much time on my hands
the stars rekindling old dreams
of her eyes
whispering into my soul
the back alley screams of passion
recollecting scenes of lust from my past
cars drive by
the neon lights blitz my head
i want to jump
drive a stake through this heart
see if i can fly
show the world what murder really is
but i succumb to fear
dreams of someone else
some fucked up thought that
everything happens for a reason
i'll grow from this
soon i'll be inward
withdrawn
drinking uncontrollably
smoking three packs a day
watching old films of bogart
polishing my guns
peeking through the window
hoping to see the sun
women
laughter of children
only to see death
paranoia

hypodermic needles
marching through the streets
of los angeles
the roaches break through the wall
of my existence
they crawl on my skin
have sex
eat/drink
get into long conversations
about the national debt
i can feel them killing me
nibbling at this tattered skin
soon i'm nothing but
old bones
broken dreams
a burning cigarette resting
at the base of my soul
i wonder who'll bring
the gasoline

within five minutes of entering the supermarket

standing in the beer
aisle wondering if the
imported shit is really
worth four extra dollars
when this attractive
black woman fell to
the floor

my first inclination
was to laugh

my mom of course
rushed over to see if
she was alright as the
woman was blaming
her heels and diabetes
for the fall

i settled for domestic

later in the fruits and
vegetables section this
little kid said hello to
me but he didn't use
my name or mister

he said hello to the
big fat guy

i laughed and thought
about karma

and the more i thought
about it the more i
wanted to teach that
kid how much the
truth really hurts

but i refrained
figured life would
get to him soon
enough

yet another pitiful display

old songs
on the radio

window
cracked
open

waiting for
the phone
to ring

an old friend
visited me
yesterday and
suddenly i'm
the little boy
that's afraid he
can never be
loved enough

if there ever
was a time for
tragedy…

you can only watch the same movie so many times

i see you're rushing
toward another brush
with an over the
counter suicide

and quite frankly i've
lost all my desire to
fight with you over it

with that said

may death grant you all
the wishes life couldn't

we'll meet again
someday

probably soon

your wall of regret

it's a quiet heartbreak
at dinner alone

a fading moon casts a
bloody shadow on
your wall of regret

it's pointless to replay
the past yet you enjoy
the misery of pressing
rewind

a past that drives you
under the covers

a past that you hide
from in shame

a past that sends you
searching for the
warm end of a gun

all the while i still
believe my love for
you exists for a reason

but anytime i try to
express that you run
off to swim with the
shallow end of the
gene pool

perhaps one day one
of us will come to our
senses

being an old romantic

most of my senses have
been grinded to dust

spit out by the masses
of beauty queens still
waiting for something
better

J.J. Campbell lives, writes and hopefully will die one day on his family farm in Ohio. An avid lover of sports, music and pornography, J.J. was first published at the age of 19. Now in his mid 30's, he is the author of many chapbooks and broadsides. *Sofisticated White Trash* is his first full length book of poems. J.J. can be found on most days in front of his computer, maintaining his blog or teaching himself to play chess. He hopes to one day silence the voices in his head and actually enjoy what others call living.

The author gratefully acknowledges the following publications where many of these poems first appeared. Driver's Side Airbag, Heeltap, mojo risin', First Class, Rainbow Reaper, The Blind Man's Review, Fearless, Indigo, Joey and The Blackboots, Nerve Cowboy, Remark, Babel Magazine, Potty Mouth Press, Phony Lid Books, Kitty Litter Press, Pink Anarchkitty Press, Failed Seeker, Thunder Sandwich, Unlikely Stories, aggressivebehavior anthologyone, Zygote in My Coffee, Underground Voices, Antipatico, The Dublin Quarterly, Chiron Review, Half Drunk Muse, St. Vitus Press & Poetry Review, Scintillating Publications, Prose Ax, My Favorite Bullet, Naked Knuckle, The Circle Magazine, EastVillagePoetry.com, Gunch Press, Instant Pussy, Concrete Meat Sheet, GPP Reader, Cherry Bleeds, Zen Baby, The Commonline Project, Opium Poetry 2.0, Propaganda Press, ZYX, FUCK!, ART:Mag, The Panulaan Review, The Joint, abandoned blog, Gutter Eloquence Magazine, Asphodel Madness 2.0, Horror Sleaze Trash

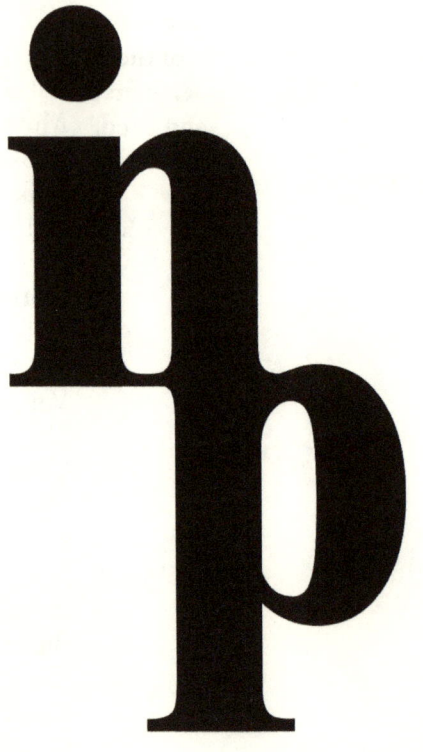

www.interiornoisepress.com

www.ingramcontent.com/pod-product-compliance
Lightning Source LLC
Chambersburg PA
CBHW020932090426
42736CB00010B/1115